Student's Book
Stage 2

English in a quarter of the time!

The Callan ® Method was first developed and published
in 1960 by R.K.T. Callan.
This edition was published for the international market in 2012.

Copyright © R.K.T. Callan 2012

Student's Book – Stage 2
ISBN 978-1-908954-13-8

CALLAN and the CALLAN logo are registered trade marks
of Callan Works Limited, used under licence by Callan Publishing Limited

Printed in the EU

Conditions of sale

All rights reserved. No part of this publication may be reproduced, stored in a retrieval system or transmitted in any form or by any means, electronic, mechanical, photocopying, recording or otherwise, without the prior permission of the publishers.

This book is sold subject to the condition that it shall not by way of trade or otherwise be lent, re-sold, hired out or otherwise circulated without the publisher's prior consent in any form of binding or cover other than that in which it is published and without a similar condition including this condition being imposed on the subsequent purchaser.

Published by

CALLAN PUBLISHING LTD.
Orchard House, 45-47 Mill Way, Grantchester, Cambridge CB3 9ND
in association with CALLAN METHOD ORGANISATION LTD.

www.callan.co.uk

- Para obtener la traducción de este prefacio en español, visitar
  www.callan.co.uk/preface/es

- Per una traduzione di questa prefazione in Italiano, visitare il sito
  www.callan.co.uk/preface/it

- Para obter uma tradução deste prefácio em português, visite
  www.callan.co.uk/preface/pt

- Z polskim tłumaczeniem tego wstępu można zapoznać się na stronie
  www.callan.co.uk/preface/pl

- Pour obtenir la traduction de cette préface en français, rendez-vous sur le site
  www.callan.co.uk/preface/fr

- Bu önsözün Türkçe çevirisi için aşağıdaki web adresini ziyaret edin
  www.callan.co.uk/preface/tr

- 本序言的中文翻译，请访问
  www.callan.co.uk/preface/ch

- 前書きの日本語版の翻訳は次ページをご覧ください
  www.callan.co.uk/preface/jp

- للاطلاع على ترجمة هذه المقدمة باللغة العربية يرجي زيارة
  www.callan.co.uk/preface/ar

Welcome to the Callan Method

Learning English with the Callan™ Method is fast and effective!

The Callan Method is a teaching method created specifically to improve your English in an intensive atmosphere. The teacher is constantly asking questions, so you are hearing and using the language as much as possible. When you speak in the lesson, the teacher corrects your grammar and pronunciation mistakes, and you learn a lot from this correction.

The Callan Method teaches English vocabulary and grammar in a carefully programmed way, with systematic revision and reinforcement. In the lesson, there is a lot of speaking and listening practice, but there is also reading and writing so that you revise and consolidate what you have learned.

With the Callan Method, the teacher speaks quickly so that you learn to understand English when it is spoken at natural speed. This also means that everyone is concentrating hard all the time.

English in a quarter of the time

The Callan Method can teach English in a quarter of the time taken by any other method on the market. Instead of the usual 350 hours necessary to get the average student to the level of the Cambridge Preliminary English Test (PET), the Callan Method can take as little as 80 hours, and only 160 hours for the Cambridge First Certificate in English (FCE).

The method is suitable for students of all nationalities, and ages. It requires no equipment (not even a whiteboard) or other books, and can be used for classes at private schools, state schools and universities. It is also possible for students to use the books to practise with each other when they are not at school.

In addition to this, students can practise their English online using the interactive exercises, which are available to students who study at licensed schools. Ask your school for details.

The Callan Method in practice

A Callan Method English lesson is probably very different from lessons you have done in the past. You do not sit in silence, doing a reading comprehension test or a grammar exercise from a book. You do not have 'free conversation', where you only use the English you already feel comfortable with. Of course, activities like this can help you, but you can do them at home with a book, or in a coffee bar. In a Callan Method lesson, you are busy with important activities that you cannot do outside the classroom. You are listening to English all the time. You are speaking English a lot, and all your mistakes are corrected. You learn quickly because you are always surrounded by English. There is no silence and no time to get bored or lose your concentration. And it is also fun!

So, what exactly happens in a Callan Method lesson, and how does it work?

The teacher asks you questions

The Callan Method books are full of questions. Each question practises a word, an expression, or a piece of grammar. The teacher is standing, and asks the questions to the students one by one. You never know when the teacher will ask you, so you are always concentrating. When one student finishes answering one question, the teacher immediately starts to ask the next question.

The teacher speaks quickly

The teacher in a Callan Method lesson speaks quickly. This is because, in the real world, it is natural to speak quickly. If you want to understand normal English, you must practise listening to quick natural speech and become able to understand English without first translating into your language. This idea of not translating is at the centre of the Callan Method; this method helps you to start thinking in English.

Also, we do not want you to stop and think a lot about the grammar while you are speaking. We want you to speak as a reflex, instinctively. And do not worry about mistakes. You will, naturally, make a lot of mistakes in the lessons, but Callan Method teachers correct your mistakes, and you learn from the corrections. When you go home, of course it will help if you read your book, think about the grammar, study the vocabulary, and do all the things that language students do at home – but the lessons are times to practise your listening and speaking, with your books closed!

The teacher says every question twice, and helps you with the answer

In the lesson, the teacher speaks quickly, so we say the questions twice. This way, you have another chance to listen if you did not understand everything the first time.

The teacher then immediately says the beginning of the answer. This is to help you (and 'push' you) to start speaking immediately. So, for example:

Teacher: *"Are there two chairs in this room? Are there two chairs in this room? No, there aren't ..."*

Student (immediately): *"No, there aren't two chairs in this room; there are twelve chairs in this room."*

If the teacher does not 'push' you by giving you the beginning of the answer, you might start to think too much, and translate into your language.

The teacher will speak along with you all the time while you are saying your answer. So, if you forget a word or you are not sure what to say, you will always hear the next word or two from the teacher. You should repeat after the teacher, but immediately try again to continue with the answer yourself. You must always try to continue speaking, and only copy the teacher when you cannot continue alone. That way, you will become more confident and learn more quickly. Never simply wait for help from the teacher and then copy – you will not improve so quickly.

Long answers, with the same grammar as the question

We want you to practise your speaking as much as possible, so you always make complete sentences when you speak in the lesson, using the same grammatical structure as in the question. For example:

Teacher: *"About how many pages are there in this book?"*

Student: *"There are about two hundred pages in that book."*

In this way, you are not just answering a question; you are making full sentences with the vocabulary and the grammar that you need to learn.

Correction by imitation

With the Callan Method, the teacher corrects all your mistakes the moment you make them. The teacher corrects you by imitating (copying) your mistake and then saying the correct pronunciation/form of the word. For example, if you say "He come from Spain", the teacher quickly says "not come - **comes**". This correction by imitation helps you to hear the difference between your mistake and the proper English form. You should immediately repeat the correct word and continue with your sentence. You learn a lot from this correction of your mistakes, and constant correction results in fast progress.

Contracted forms

In the lesson, the teacher uses contractions (e.g. the teacher says "I don't" instead of "I do not"). This is because it is natural to use contractions in spoken English and you must learn to understand them. Also, if you want to sound natural when you speak, you must learn to use contractions.

Lesson structure

Every school is different, but a typical 50-minute Callan lesson will contain about 35 minutes of speaking, a 10-minute period for reading, and a 5-minute dictation. The reading practice and the dictation are often in the middle of the lesson.

In the reading part, you read and speak while the teacher helps you and corrects your mistakes. In the dictation, you practise your writing, but you are also listening to the teacher. So, a 50-minute Callan lesson is 50 minutes of spoken English with no silence!

No chatting

Although the Callan Method emphasises the importance of speaking practice, this does not mean chatting (free conversation). You learn English quickly with the Callan Method partly because the lessons are organised, efficient, fast and busy. There is no time wasted on chatting; this can be done before or after the lesson.

Chatting is not a good way to spend your time in an English lesson. First, only some of the students speak. Second, in a chat, people only use the English that they already know. Third, it is difficult for a teacher to correct mistakes during a conversation.

The Callan Method has none of these problems. All through the lesson, every student is listening and speaking, practising different vocabulary and structures, and learning from the correction of their mistakes. And nobody has time to get bored!

Repeat, repeat, repeat!

Systematic revision

In your native language, you sometimes read or hear a word that you do not already know. You usually need to read or hear this new word only once or twice in order to remember it and then use it yourself. However, when you are learning a foreign language, things are very different. You need to hear, see and use words and grammatical structures many times before you really know them properly. So your studies must involve a system of revision (repeating what you have studied before). This is absolutely essential. If there is no system of revision in your studies, you will forget what you have studied and will not be able to speak or understand better than before.

In every Callan Method lesson, of course you learn new English, practise it, and progress through your book. However, you also do a lot of revision so that you can really learn what you have studied. Your teacher can decide how much revision your class needs, but it will always be an important part of your studies.

Also, because there is a lot of revision, it is not important for you to understand everything the first time; it gets easier. The revision with Callan is automatic and systematic. Every day you do a lot of revision and then learn some new English.

Revision in reading and dictation too

The reading and dictation practice in the lessons is part of Callan's systematic revision as well. First, you learn a new word in the speaking part of the lesson; a few lessons later, you meet it again when you are reading; finally, the word appears in a dictation. This is all written into the Callan Method; it happens automatically.

Correcting your dictations

With the Callan Method, there is little or no homework to do, but it is very important that you correct your dictations. These are printed in your book and so you can easily correct them at home, on the bus, or wherever. It is important to do this because it helps you to learn the written forms of the words you have already studied in earlier lessons.

Your first lessons with the Callan Method

During your first lesson with the Callan Method, all of the questions and some of the vocabulary are new for you; you have not done any revision yet. For this reason, the teacher may not ask you many questions. You can sit and listen, and become more familiar with the method - the speed, the questions, the correction etc.

History of the Callan Method – Robin Callan

Robin Callan is the creator of the Callan Method. He owns the Callan School in London's Oxford Street. He also runs Callan Publishing Limited, which supplies Callan Method books to schools all over the world.

Robin Callan grew up in Ely, Cambridgeshire, England. In his early twenties, he went to Italy to teach English in Salerno. Although he enjoyed teaching, Robin thought that the way in which teachers were expected to teach their lessons was inefficient and boring. He became very interested in the mechanisms of language learning, and was sure that he could radically improve the way English was taught.

He remained in Italy and started to write his own books for teaching English. He used these in his own classes and, over the following ten years, gained an immense amount of practical experience and a reputation for teaching English quickly and effectively.

When he returned to England, he opened his school in Oxford Street. As the method became more and more popular with students, the school grew and moved to larger premises. Robin continued to write his Callan Method books, and today the method is used by schools all over the world.

Robin Callan has always been passionate about English literature, especially poetry. For this reason, he bought The Orchard Tea Garden in Grantchester, near Cambridge, which attracts thousands of tourists each year. Throughout the 20th century, it was a popular meeting place for many famous Cambridge University students and important figures from English literature, such as Rupert Brooke, Virginia Woolf and E.M. Forster. Today, it is also home to the Rupert Brooke Museum.

Mr Callan now lives in Grantchester, but still plays an active role in the management of the Callan School in London.

The Callan School in London's Oxford Street

The largest private school in London

The Callan School in Oxford Street is the largest private school in London teaching English as a foreign language. Depending on the time of year, the school employs between 60 and 100 teachers and has an average of 1600 students passing through its doors every day. This number rises to more than 2000 in the middle of summer, similar to a small university.

Websites

Please visit the following websites for more information:

Callan Method http://www.callan.co.uk
Lots of information, including a list of schools around the world that use the method

Callan School London http://www.callanschoollondon.com/en/callan-school
All you need to know about the largest private English language school in London

How Callan Method Stages compare to CEFR* levels and University of Cambridge General English exams

Common European Framework of Reference

It is difficult to compare the Callan Method books directly with the CEFR levels and Cambridge exams, but below is an approximate guide.

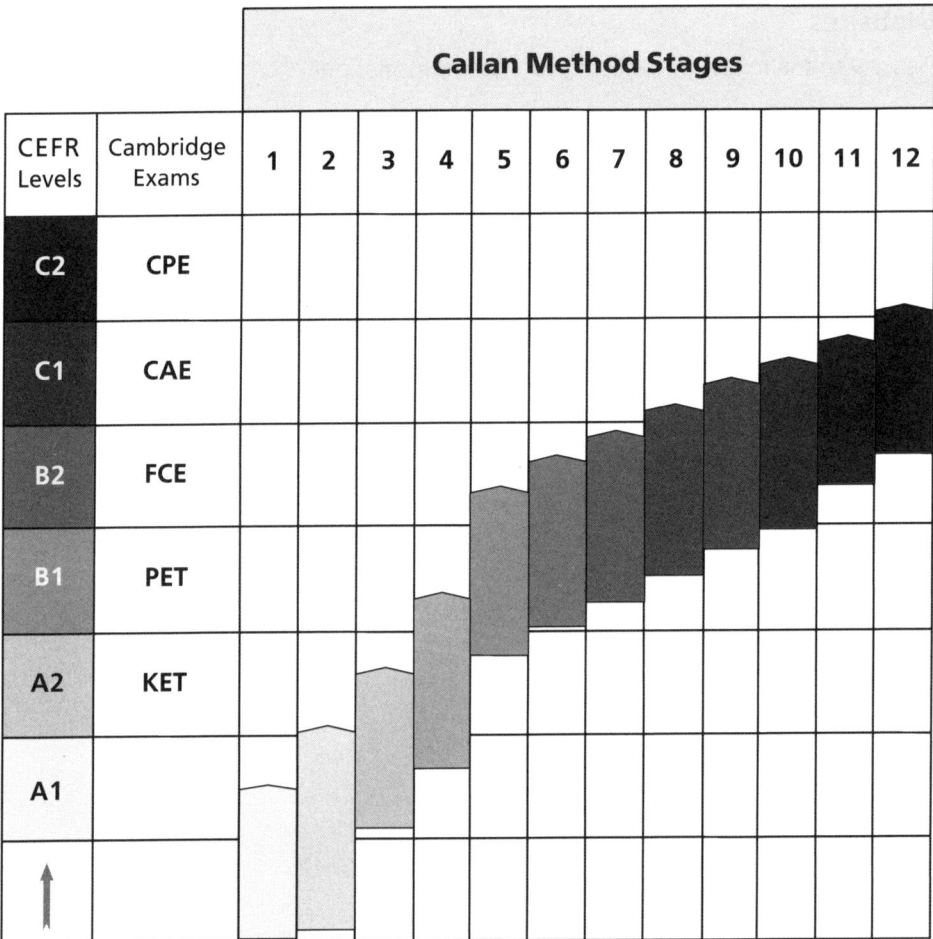

STAGE 2

LESSON 10

53  *See Chart 5*

Present continuous

| home | speak | that |

Present continuous (positive)

I	am	
you	are	
he		
she	is	speaking
it		
we		
you	are	
they		

We use the present continuous for an action that we are doing now. For example, I am going to the door; I am coming from the door; I am closing the book; I am opening the book.

Wot am au duing?

54 What am I doing? — You're opening the book

What am I doing? — You're closing the book

What am I doing? — You're going to the door

Are you speaking English? — Yes, I'm speaking English

Is he/she sitting on a chair? — Yes, he's/she's sitting on a chair

Present continuous (negative)

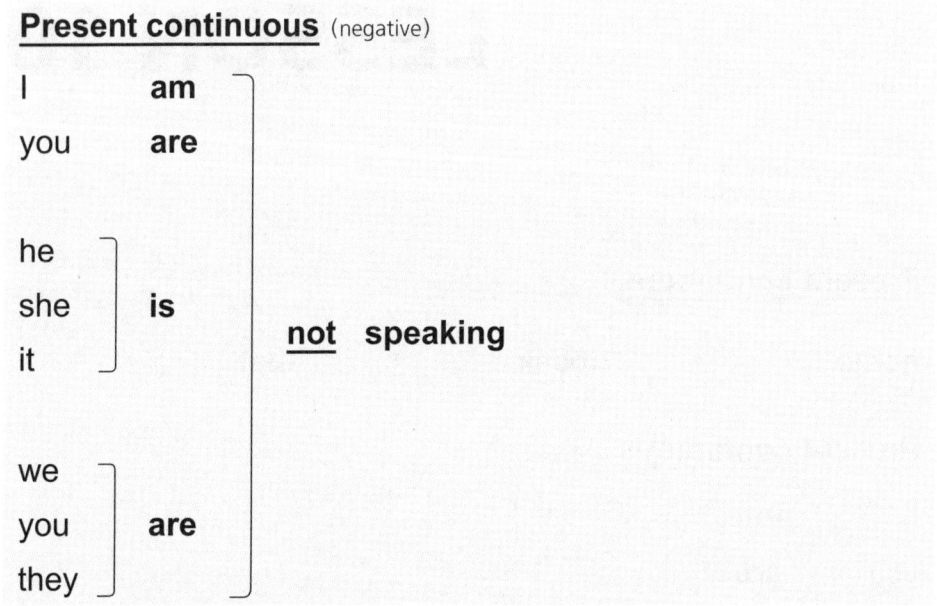

For the negative, we say "not". For example, I am not speaking French; you are not standing on the table.

55 Am I writing in the book? No, you aren't writing in the book; you're reading the book

Are you speaking ... (student's language)? No, I'm not speaking ...; I'm speaking English

Is he standing on the floor? No, he isn't standing on the floor; he's sitting on the chair

Is she speaking French? No, she isn't speaking French; she's speaking English

Are we going home? No, we aren't going home; we're remaining in the room

Are they standing behind the house? No, they aren't standing behind the house; they're standing in front of the house

Present continuous (questions)

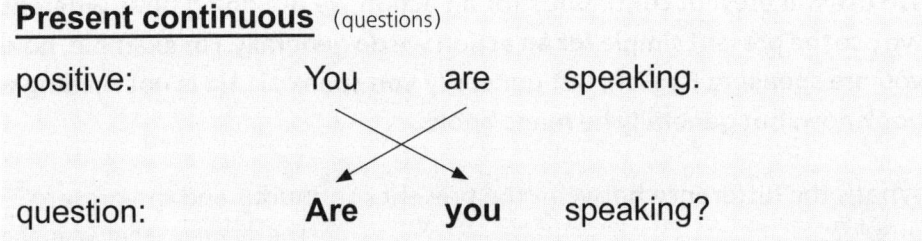

"You are speaking" is a positive sentence. For a question, we put "are" before "you" and we say "Are you speaking?"

Are you sitting on a chair?   Yes, I'm sitting on a chair

What am I doing?   You're closing the book

56 Ask him/her a question with the present continuous.
                                        What are you doing? Am I writing? etc.

 *See Chart 5*

Present simple	do	does
Japanese	Chinese	

Present simple (positive)

I
you } **speak**

he
she } **speak<u>s</u>**
it

we
you } **speak**
they

We use the present continuous for an action we are doing now, whereas we use the present simple for an action we do generally. For example, now you are speaking English, but generally you speak … . He is not reading a book now, but generally he reads books.

57 What's the difference between the present continuous and the present simple?

> The difference between the present continuous and the present simple is that we use the present continuous for an action we are doing now, whereas we use the present simple for an action we do generally

With the present simple, we use the word "do". The word "do" hasn't got a meaning, but we use it in questions and negative sentences. For example, we say "Do you speak Japanese?" and "You do not speak Japanese".

Are you reading that book?	No, I'm not reading this book
Do you read that book?	Yes, I read this book
Are you writing?	No, I'm not writing
Do you write?	Yes, I write
Am I going to the door?	No, you aren't going to the door; you're remaining on the chair
Do I go to the door after the lesson?	Yes, you go to the door after the lesson

For "he", "she" and "it", we use the word "does". For example, we say "Does he speak Japanese?" and "He does not speak Japanese".

Is he going home?	No, he isn't going home; he's remaining in the room
Does he go home after the lesson?	Yes, he goes home after the lesson

58 Is she speaking? — No, she isn't speaking

Does she speak? — Yes, she speaks

do not	don't	
does not	doesn't	remain

Present simple (negative)

I, you — **do not speak**

he, she, it — **does not speak**

we, you, they — **do not speak**

For the negative of the present simple, we use the words "do not" and we say "I do not speak Chinese". The contraction of "do not" is "don't" – "I don't speak Chinese".

What's the negative of "I speak"?	The negative of "I speak" is "I don't speak"
Do you remain here after the lesson?	No, I don't remain here after the lesson; I go home
Do they speak Japanese?	No, they don't speak Japanese; they speak …
Do I read books in Chinese?	No, you don't read books in Chinese; you read books in English

For "he", "she" and "it", we use the words "does not" for the negative, and we say "He does not speak Chinese". The contraction of "does not" is "doesn't" – "He doesn't speak Chinese".

What's the negative of "he speaks"?   The negative of "he speaks" is "he doesn't speak"

Does he/she speak Japanese?   No, he/she doesn't speak Japanese; he/she speaks ...

Does he/she remain here after the lesson?   No, he/she doesn't remain here after the lesson; he/she goes home after the lesson

Does he/she write in German?   No, he/she doesn't write in German; he/she writes in ...

Present simple (questions)

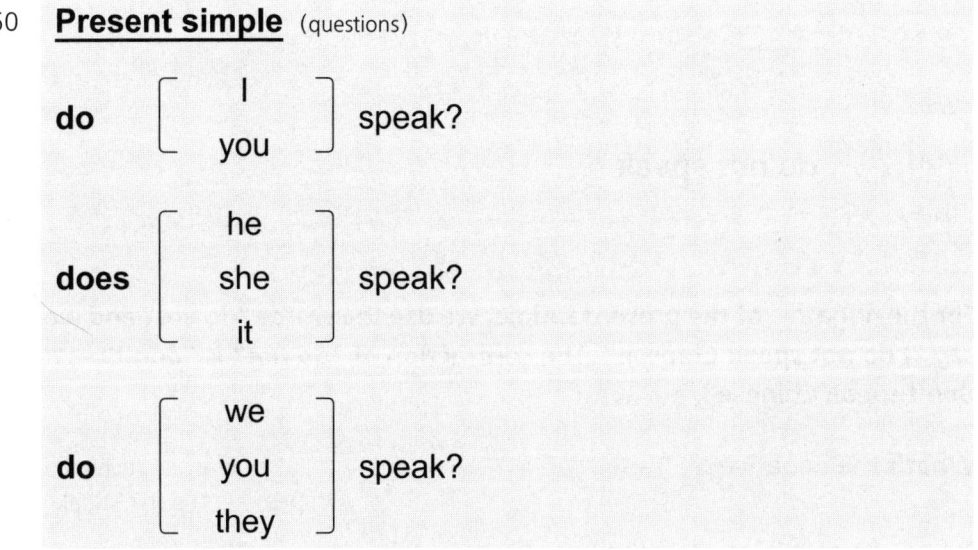

For questions, we use the words "do" and "does", and we say "Do you speak Chinese?" or "Does she write in German?"

Ask him/her a question with the word "do", please.
Do you speak English? Do they read their books at home?

Ask him/her a question with the word "does", please.
Does he speak Chinese? Does she read books in French?

 *Dictation 2*

You aren't Mrs Brown;/ you're Mr Green./ I'm Mrs Brown./ Six, seven, eight,/ nine, ten./ The women/ are standing/ under the light/ in front of/ the picture./ Where's the house?/ It's behind her./ What am I doing?/ You're taking the bag/ from me,/ closing it,/ and putting it/ on the floor./ Which door/ is open?/ That door is./ Eleven, twelve, thirteen,/ fourteen, fifteen.

LESSON 11

62 **about**   **page**

About how many people are there in your country?   There are about ... people in my country

About how many things are there in this room?   There are about ... things in this room

About how many pages are there in this book?   There are about ... pages in that book

can

Can you speak ...?   Yes, I can speak ...

Can you touch that book?   Yes, I can touch that (or this) book

Can you read and write?   Yes, I can read and write

like   **dislike**   **cinema**   **television**

Do you like your city (or town or village)?   Yes, I like my city ~ No, I don't like my city

63 Do you dislike the cinema?   No, I don't dislike the cinema; I like the cinema

Do you like that picture?   Yes, I like that picture ~ No, I don't like that picture; I dislike that picture

Do you dislike television?   No, I don't dislike television; I like television

Does he/she dislike television?   No, he/she doesn't dislike television; he/she likes television

right   **left**

Which hand's this?   It's your left hand

Which hand's this?   It's your right hand

Put your right hand on that book, please.

What's he/she doing?   He/She is putting his/her right hand on that book

Close your left eye, please.

What's he/she doing?   He/She is closing his/her left eye

moving   still   completely

Is my hand moving?   No, your hand isn't moving; it's still

Am I standing still?   No, you aren't standing still; you're moving

Are all the parts of your body still now?   No, not all the parts of my body are still now; my mouth and my tongue etc. are moving

Do you generally sit completely still in the lesson?   No, I don't generally sit completely still in the lesson; I move

Does he/she generally sit completely still in the lesson?   No, he/she doesn't generally sit completely still in the lesson; he/she moves

wearing   wear   glasses

What clothes are you wearing?   I'm wearing shoes, socks, a suit, etc.

Are you wearing glasses?   Yes, I'm wearing glasses ~ No, I'm not wearing glasses

Are you wearing a hat?   No, I'm not wearing a hat

Do you wear a hat?   Yes, I wear a hat

Are you wearing a coat?   No, I'm not wearing a coat

Do you wear a coat?   Yes, I wear a coat

with

What am I doing?	You're touching your nose with your finger
Do we speak with our mouths?	Yes, we speak with our mouths
Do we read with our eyes?	Yes, we read with our eyes

half

How much is half of a hundred?	Fifty is half of a hundred
How much is half of thirteen?	Six and a half is half of thirteen
Are half of the people in this town men?	Yes, half of the people in this town are men

tell

Tell me your name, please.	My name's ...
What's he/she doing?	He/She is telling you his/her name
Tell me the name of the capital of Russia, please.	Moscow's the capital of Russia
What's he/she doing?	He/She is telling you the name of the capital of Russia

LESSON 12

66
Russian	**Greek**
Are you (Russian) or (Greek)?	No, I'm not (Russian) or (Greek); I'm ...
Do you speak (Greek)?	No, I don't speak (Greek); I speak ...

prefer	**tea**	**coffee**

Which do you prefer: <u>the</u> cinema or television?	I prefer ... to ...
Which do you prefer: tea or coffee?	I prefer ... to ...
Which does he/she prefer: tea or coffee?	He/She prefers ... to ...
Do the English generally prefer coffee?	No, the English don't generally prefer coffee; they generally prefer tea

both

We use "both" for two people or things. Both my hands are on the table. Both of us are in the room. We aren't both sitting; you're sitting, but I'm standing.

Are both my hands on the table?	Yes, both your hands are on the table
Are both these books open?	Yes, both these books are open

67 We can say "both chairs" or "both of the chairs" but, with the words "us", "you" and "them", we say "both <u>of</u> us/you/them" and not "both us/you/them".

Which is it right to say: "both us" or "both <u>of</u> us"?	It's right to say "both <u>of</u> us"
Are both of you sitting?	Yes, both of us are sitting

Do both of them speak English?	Yes, both of them speak English
Are both of us speaking English?	Yes, both of us are speaking English
Are we both sitting?	No, we aren't both sitting; I'm sitting, but you're standing

mean   hello   goodbye   thank you

What does the word "hello" mean in …?	The word "hello" means "…" in …
What does the word "goodbye" mean in …?	The word "goodbye" means "…" in …
What do the words "thank you" mean in …?	The words "thank you" mean "…" in …

language   European   Asian   Germany

Which language are we speaking now?	We're speaking English now
Which language do you generally speak?	I generally speak …
Which language does he/she generally speak?	He/she generally speaks …
Is Chinese a European language?	No, Chinese isn't a European language; it's an Asian language
Is Germany an Asian country?	No, Germany isn't an Asian country; it's a European country

I	have not		I	haven't
you	have not		you	haven't
he	has not		he	hasn't
she	has not		she	hasn't
it	has not		it	hasn't
we	have not		we	haven't
you	have not		you	haven't
they	have not		they	haven't

only

The negative of "I have" is "I have not", and the contraction is "I haven't".

69 What's the negative of "I have"?
The negative of "I have" is "I have not"

What's the contraction of "I have not"?
The contraction of "I have not" is "I haven't"

Have I got four arms?
No, you haven't got four arms; you've only got two arms

Have you got two heads?
No, I haven't got two heads; I've only got one head

Has he only got one hand?
No, he hasn't only got one hand; he's got two hands

Has she got two noses?
No, she hasn't got two noses; she's only got one nose

Have we only got one mouth?
No, we haven't only got one mouth; we've got two mouths (i.e. you and the student)

Have they got eight ears?
No, they haven't got eight ears; they've only got four ears

the same ... as   different ... from   Japan

Are your shoes the same as my shoes?
No, my shoes aren't the same as your shoes; they're different from your shoes

Are the French the same as the Russians? *(Pagunks)*
No, the French aren't the same as the Russians; they're different from the Russians

70 Are your eyes the same colour as my eyes?
Yes, my eyes are the same colour as your eyes ~ No, my eyes aren't the same colour as your eyes; they're a different colour from your eyes

Do the people in Germany speak the same language as the people in Japan?
No, the people in Germany don't speak the same language as the people in Japan; they speak a different language from the people in Japan

Which is it right to say: "people are" or "people is"?   It's right to say "people are"

 *Dictation 3*

Who are they?/ They're Mr and Mrs Long./ The plural of "man"/ is "men"./ The plural of "woman"/ is "women"./ The boots are/ under that chair./ These windows are red and blue;/ those are yellow and grey./ Sixteen, seventeen, eighteen,/ nineteen, twenty./ The letters/ of the alphabet/ are: ABC – DEF – GHI – JKL – MNO – PQR – STU – VWX – YZ./ A is before B/ and J is after I./ E is between/ D and F.

LESSON 13

71  *See Chart 4*

anybody? non-specific	**somebody**
	not anybody
who? specific	Mrs Brown Mr Smith etc.
	nobody

Both "anybody" and "somebody" mean "...". We use "anybody" in questions and negative sentences, and "somebody" in positive sentences. For example, we say "Is there anybody sitting here? Yes, there's somebody sitting here. Is there anybody sitting there? No, there isn't anybody sitting there". "Anybody" is non-specific and has a non-specific answer, whereas "who" is specific and has a specific answer – "Mrs Brown", "Mr Smith" etc., or "nobody".

What do the words "anybody" and "somebody" mean?   The words "anybody" and "somebody" mean ...

What's the difference between "anybody" and "somebody"?   The difference between "anybody" and "somebody" is that we use "anybody" in questions and negative sentences, whereas we use "somebody" in positive sentences

anybody

Is there anybody in this room?   Yes, there's somebody in this room

72 Is there anybody speaking to you?   Yes, there's somebody speaking to me

Is there anybody sitting there on that chair?	Yes, there's somebody sitting there on that chair

not anybody   **corridor**

Is there anybody sitting on the floor?	No, there isn't anybody sitting on the floor
Is there anybody in this room wearing a hat?	No, there isn't anybody in this room wearing a hat
Is there anybody in the corridor?	No, there isn't anybody in the corridor

nobody

Who's speaking English in this room?	We're speaking English in this room
Who's speaking (French) in this room?	Nobody's speaking (French) in this room
Who's wearing clothes in this room?	We're wearing clothes in this room
Who's wearing a hat in this room?	Nobody's wearing a hat in this room
Who's giving you an English lesson?	You're giving me an English lesson
Who's in the corridor?	Nobody's in the corridor

73 **walk**

What am I doing?	You're walking
Where am I walking to?	You're walking to the window
Do you like walking?	Yes, I like walking
Does he/she like walking?	Yes, he/she likes walking

Mr Brown's

We prefer to say "Mr Brown's suit" and not "the suit of Mr Brown".

Is this Mr Brown's dress?	No, it isn't Mr Brown's dress; it's Mrs Brown's dress
Is this Mr Brown's shirt?	Yes, it's Mr Brown's shirt
Is this Mr Brown's arm?	No, it isn't Mr Brown's arm; it's Mrs Brown's arm
Is this Mr Smith's ear?	No, it isn't Mr Smith's ear; it's Mr Brown's ear
Is this ...'s book?	No, it isn't ...'s book; it's ...'s book

stand up   sit down   up   down

What's my right hand doing?	Your right hand's moving up and down
What am I doing?	You're sitting down
What am I doing?	You're standing up
Do you sit down after the lesson?	No, I don't sit down after the lesson; I stand up after the lesson

cannot   can't

The negative of "can" is "cannot", and the contraction of "cannot" is "can't".

What's the negative of "can"?	The negative of "can" is "cannot"
What's the contraction of "cannot"?	The contraction of "cannot" is "can't"
Can you speak (Chinese)?	No, I can't speak (Chinese)

Can you put the table into your pocket?	No, I can't put the table into my pocket
Can you touch the ceiling?	No, I can't touch the ceiling

75 **quarter**

How much is a quarter of forty?	Ten is a quarter of forty
How much is a quarter of a thousand?	250 is a quarter of a thousand
What's a quarter of ten?	Two-and-a-half is a quarter of ten
What's a quarter of five?	One-and-a-quarter is a quarter of five

teach   **learn**   **Spanish**

Are you teaching me English?	No, I'm not teaching you English; I'm learning English from you
Do you learn Spanish?	No, I don't learn Spanish; I learn English
Do you like learning a language?	Yes, I like learning a language
Does he/she like learning a language?	Yes, he/she likes learning a language

LESSON 14

76   **easy**   **difficult**   **grammar**

Is English grammar difficult?
    No, English grammar isn't difficult; it's easy

Is Chinese an easy language to learn?
    No, Chinese isn't an easy language to learn; it's a difficult language to learn

Is it difficult for you to speak your language?
    No, it isn't difficult for me to speak my language; it's easy

Is it generally easy for people to write with their left hand?
    No, it isn't generally easy for people to write with their left hand; it's difficult

hang   **map**

What's my pen doing?
    Your pen's hanging between your finger and your thumb

Is there a light hanging from the ceiling?
    Yes, there's a light hanging from the ceiling ~ No, there isn't a light hanging from the ceiling

Is there a map hanging on that wall?
    Yes, there's a map hanging on that wall ~ No, there isn't a map hanging on that wall

77   **by**   **car**   **bus**   **train**   **school**

Do you go home after the lesson by car, by bus, by train or do you walk home?
    I go home after the lesson by ... ~I walk home after the lesson; I don't go by car, by bus or by train

Which do you prefer: to walk or go by car?
    I prefer to ...

Do you come to school by train or by bus?
    I come to school by ...

Does he/she come to school by train or by bus? — He/She comes to school by …

married **single** **Miss**

Are you married? — Yes, I'm married ~ No, I'm not married; I'm single

Is Mr Brown single? — No, Mr Brown isn't single; he's married

Is Miss Brown married? — No, Miss Brown isn't married; she's single

husband **wife**

Has Mr Brown got a wife? — Yes, Mr Brown's got a wife

Has Mrs Brown got a husband? — Yes, Mrs Brown's got a husband

Is Mrs Brown's husband standing behind the house? — No, Mrs Brown's husband isn't standing behind the house; he's standing in front of the house

mother **father**

What's your mother's name? — My mother's name is …

What's your father's name? — My father's name is …

What's your father's wife's name? — My father's wife's name is …

What's your mother's husband's name? — My mother's husband's name is …

child **children** **only child**

What's the plural of "child"? — The plural of "child" is "children"

How many children have your mother and father got? — My mother and father have got … child/children

Are you an only child? — Yes, I'm an only child ~ No, I'm not an only child

call   mum   dad

What do we call this? | We call this an arm (or a handkerchief, a leg etc.)

79 What do we call the people in France? | We call the people in France French

What do we call the thing we wear on our heads? | We call the thing we wear on our heads a hat

What do people generally call their mother and father? | People generally call their mother and father "Mum" and "Dad"

one ... the other

Are both my hands on the table? | No, both your hands aren't on the table; one's on the table and the other's on your arm

Are both my hands closed? | No, both your hands aren't closed; one's closed and the other's open

Are both these pencils red? | No, both these pencils aren't red; one's red and the other's grey

kind

What's this? | It's a book

What kind of book is this? | It's an English book

What kind of room is this? | It's a classroom

What kind of car do you prefer? | I prefer ...

 *Dictation 4*

We are/ in front of them,/ and they are/ behind us./ There are/ five vowels/ in the English alphabet:/ A, E, I, O, U./ I'm the teacher/ and you're the student./ Thirty, forty, fifty,/ sixty, seventy,/ eighty, ninety,/ a hundred, a thousand,/ a million./ Thirty plus thirteen/ equals forty-three./ There's a shoe/ on the floor./ This is/ not a sock/ or a jacket;/ it's a suit./ Now put the book here,/ please.

 *Do Revision Exercise 2*

LESSON 15

81 Preposition

The words "on", "under", "in", "from" etc. are prepositions.

Give me some examples of prepositions, please.
    Some examples of prepositions are "on", "under", "in" and "from"

Where do you come from?
    I come from ...

Where do I come from?
    You come from ...

When we use question words, for example "what", "which" and "where", we put the preposition last in the sentence. For example, we do not say "From where do you come?"; we say "Where do you come from?" We do not say "On what are you putting the book?"; we say "What are you putting the book on?"

What do we speak with?
    We speak with our mouths

Where am I taking the book from?
    You're taking the book from the table

What am I putting the pen under?
    You're putting the pen under the book

What are you sitting on?
    I'm sitting on a chair

82

north   south   east   west

cardinal point   Paris

Tell me the names of the four cardinal points, please.
    The names of the four cardinal points are north, south, east and west

Is Greece west of Italy?
    No, Greece isn't west of Italy; it's east of Italy

Is Paris in the south of France?	No, Paris isn't in the south of France; it's in the north of France
Is Germany east or west of Italy?	Germany isn't east or west of Italy; it's north of Italy

place   some of

How many places are there in this room?	There are ... places in this room
Is there anybody sitting in that place?	Yes, there's somebody sitting in that place
Tell me the names of some of the places you like in this country?	The names of some of the places I like in this country are ...

83 opposite

What's the opposite of "high"?	The opposite of "high" is "low"
What's the opposite of "behind"?	The opposite of "behind" is "in front of"
What's the opposite of "tall"?	The opposite of "tall" is "short"
What's the opposite of the verb "to teach"?	The opposite of the verb "to teach" is "to learn"

without

What's the opposite of "with"?	The opposite of "with" is "without"
Can we write without a pen or a pencil?	No, we can't write without a pen or a pencil
Can we speak without opening our mouths?	No, we can't speak without opening our mouths
Can you read without wearing glasses?	Yes, I can read without wearing glasses ~ No, I can't read without wearing glasses

Verb   Noun   translation

A verb is a word we use for an action. For example, "take", "put", "open", "close" etc. are verbs. A noun is the name of a thing. For example, "book", "picture", "wall" etc. are nouns. The word "translate" is a verb, whereas the word "translation" is a noun. The word "mean" is a verb, whereas the word "meaning" is a noun.

What's the difference between a verb and a noun? The difference between a verb and a noun is that a verb is a word we use for an action, whereas a noun is the name of a thing

Give me an example of a verb, please. "Take" is a verb

Give me an example of a noun. "Book" is a noun

Is the word "translation" a verb or a noun? The word "translation" is a noun

during   about

Do we speak ... during the lesson? No, we don't speak ... during the lesson; we speak English

Do you walk about the room during the lesson? No, I don't walk about the room during the lesson; I sit on my chair

Does he/she walk about the room during the lesson? No, he/she doesn't walk about the room during the lesson; he/she sits on his/her chair

About how many questions do you answer during the lesson? I answer about ... questions during the lesson

LESSON 16

85   **some ... some**

Are all the people in this town (or city or village) men?   No, not all the people in this town are men; some are men and some are women

Are all the cars in Europe Fords?   No, not all the cars in Europe are Fords; some are Fords and some are Fiats, Renaults, Volkswagens, Volvos etc.

Are all the people in this place married?   No, not all the people in this place are married; some are married and some are single

Do all the people in Europe speak Spanish?   No, not all the people in Europe speak Spanish; some speak Spanish and some speak other languages

 See Chart 4

anything?	**something**
non-specific	
	not anything
what?	a light
specific	a picture
	nothing

"Anything" and "something" both mean the same thing. We use "anything" in questions and negative sentences, and we use "something" in positive sentences. For example, we say "Have I got anything in my right hand? Yes, you've got something in your right hand. Have I got anything in my left hand? No, you haven't got anything in your left hand." "Anything" we use in a non-specific question, whereas "What?" is specific and has a specific answer – "a light, a book" etc., or "nothing".

86 anything

Have I got anything in my right hand?	Yes, you've got something in your right hand
Is there anything on the table?	Yes, there's something on the table
Are you wearing anything on your feet?	Yes, I'm wearing something on my feet

not anything

Have I got anything in my left hand?	No, you haven't got anything in your left hand
Is there anything there on the floor?	No, there isn't anything there on the floor
Are you wearing anything on your head?	No, I'm not wearing anything on my head

87 nothing

What have I got in my right hand?	You've got a pen in your right hand
What have I got in my left hand?	You've got nothing in your left hand
What's on the table?	There are some books, some pens etc. on the table
What's there on the floor?	There's nothing there on the floor
What are you wearing on your feet?	I'm wearing shoes on my feet
What are you wearing on your head?	I'm wearing nothing on my head

Only one negative

In English, in a negative sentence, we use only <u>one</u> negative word, not two. For example, we say "There is<u>n't</u> anything on this chair". A sentence with two negative words has a positive meaning. For example, "There is<u>n't</u> <u>nobody</u> on this chair" means that there <u>is</u> <u>somebody</u> on the chair. "I have <u>not</u> got <u>nothing</u> in my pocket" means that I <u>have</u> got <u>something</u> in my pocket.

Have I got anything in my hand?   Yes, you've got something in your hand

Have I got nothing in my hand?   No, you haven't got nothing in your hand; you've got something in your hand

What does this sentence mean: "I'm <u>not</u> eating <u>nothing</u>"?
"I'm not eating nothing" means "I'm eating something"

front   back   top   bottom   side

What part of the book is this?   It's the front (back, top, bottom, side) of the book

Is this the front part of my body?   No, it isn't the front part of your body; it's the back part of your body

Where's the pen?   The pen's on the top of the book

What's on the top of my head?   Your hair's on the top of your head

Are my ears on the back of my head?   No, your ears aren't on the back of your head; they're on the sides of your head

Are you sitting on my left-hand side or on my right-hand side?
I'm sitting on your ...

smell

What am I doing?   You're smelling your wrist

What do we smell with?   We smell with our noses

Has the table got any smell? — No, the table hasn't got any smell

89   address   street

What's the address of this school? — The address of this school is ... Street

What's your address? — My address is ... Street

 *Dictation 5*

The capital of England/ is not a town/ but a city./ Greece, Italy and France/ are in Europe,/ and China and India/ are in Asia./ Moscow's the capital of Russia,/ not Athens./ How much is/ thirty plus fifteen?/ There are a number of shirts,/ ties and hats/ in this room./ Those are her tights./ The cardinal numbers are/ one, two, three etc./ This is my coat.

LESSON 17

90 **many   few   match   matchbox**

Are there many people in a small village?   No, there aren't many people in a small village; there are few people in a small village

Are there few people in a large city?   No, there aren't few people in a large city; there are many people in a large city

Have you and I got many pens?   No, you and I haven't got many pens; we've got few pens

Are there few matches in a matchbox?   No, there aren't few matches in a matchbox; there are many matches in a matchbox

friend   friendly

Have you got any friends?   Yes, I've got some friends

Do you think the people in your town are friendly?   Yes, I think the people in my town are friendly ~ No, I don't think the people in my town are friendly; they're unfriendly

Are the countries of Europe generally friends now?   Yes, the countries of Europe are generally friends now

91 **into   in   that   another**

We use "into" for a thing that moves from one place to another, and "in" for a thing that remains in one place.

What am I doing?   You're putting your pen into your pocket

Where's my pen now?   Your pen's in your pocket now

What am I doing?   You're coming into the classroom

Where am I now?   You're in the classroom now

What's the difference between "into" and "in"?

> The difference between "into" and "in" is that we use "into" for a thing that moves from one place to another, and "in" for a thing that remains in one place

see   such as

What can you see in this room?   I can see many things in this room, such as some students, a table, a clock ...

Can you see him/her?   Yes, I can see him/her

Can you see anything in my left hand?   No, I can't see anything in your left hand

why   because   similar   too   Greenwich

"Why" and "because" have similar meanings, but we generally use "why" in questions and "because" in answers.

What's the difference between "why" and "because"?

> The difference between "why" and "because" is that we generally use "why" in questions and "because" in answers

Can you touch the ceiling?   No, I can't touch the ceiling

Why not?   Because the ceiling's too high for me to touch

Can you put this book into your pocket?   No, I can't put that book into my pocket

Why not?   Because that book's too large to go into my pocket

Can we call Grantchester (in England) a city?   No, we can't call Grantchester (in England) a city

Why not?   Because Grantchester is too small for us to call a city; Grantchester is a village

second   minute   hour   make

How many seconds make a minute?	Sixty seconds make a minute
How many minutes make an hour?	Sixty minutes make an hour
Can you make a suit?	Yes, I can make a suit ~ No, I can't make a suit

93 <u>Adjective</u>

The words "black", "white", "large", "small", "high", "low" etc. are adjectives. In English, we put adjectives before nouns.

Give me some examples of adjectives, please.	Some examples of adjectives are black, white, large ...
Is the word "book" an adjective?	No, the word "book" isn't an adjective; it's a noun
Which word is the adjective in this sentence: "The green pen is on the floor"?	The word "green" is the adjective in this sentence
In English, do we put an adjective before or after a noun?	In English, we put an adjective before a noun.
Give me an example, please.	a blue book; a high ceiling; an easy language

LESSON 18

94 **food**

Do you like food? — Yes, I like food

Do you like all food? — Yes, I like all food ~ No, I don't like all food; some I like and some I dislike

Do people generally dislike the smell of food? — No, people don't generally dislike the smell of food; they like the smell of food

son   **daughter**

How many sons has your dad got? — My dad's got ... son(s)

How many daughters has your mum got? — My mum's got ... daughter(s)

Are you a son or a daughter? — I'm a ...

brother   **sister**

Have you got any brothers? — Yes, I've got a/some brother(s) ~ No, I haven't got any brothers

Have you got any sisters? — Yes, I've got a/some sister(s) ~ No, I haven't got any sisters

How many brothers and sisters have you got? — I've got ...

95 **parents**   **relatives**   **relations**   **family**

uncle   **aunt**   **cousin**

What's the difference between parents and relatives? — The difference between parents and relatives is that parents are mother and father, whereas relatives are all the other people in the family, such as brothers, sisters, uncles, aunts, cousins etc.

What does the word "uncle" mean?	The word "uncle" means your mother's brother, or your father's brother
What does the word "aunt" mean?	The word "aunt" means your mother's sister, or your father's sister
What does the word "cousin" mean?	The word "cousin" means your uncle's child, or your aunt's child

more ... than

Have you got more fingers than thumbs on your hands?	Yes, I've got more fingers than thumbs on my hands
Are there more people in a town than in a village?	Yes, there are more people in a town than in a village
Are there more pages in this book than in that book?	Yes, there are more pages in this book than in that book

break

What am I doing?	You're breaking your pen
Can you break the window with a chair?	Yes, I can break the window with a chair
Can you break the table with your hands?	No, I can't break the table with my hands

out of

What am I doing?	You're putting your pen into your pocket
What am I doing?	You're taking your pen out of your pocket
What am I doing?	You're going out of the classroom
What am I doing?	You're coming into the classroom
What am I doing?	You're putting your hands into your pockets
What am I doing?	You're taking your hands out of your pockets

97   Do you go out of the classroom before the lesson?   No, I don't go out of the classroom before the lesson; I come into the classroom before the lesson

think

About how many people do you think there are in France (or Italy etc.)?   I think there are about … people in …

Do you think there's anybody in the other room?   Yes, I think there's somebody in the other room ~ No I don't think there's anybody in the other room

What do you think I've got in my pocket?   I think you've got … in your pocket

good   bad   good at   bad at

Is this a bad pen?   No, it isn't a bad pen; it's a good pen

Do you think that's a good picture?   Yes, I think that's a good picture ~ No, I don't think that's a good picture; I think it's a bad picture

Are all children good children?   No, not all children are good children; some are good and some are bad

Are all students good at learning languages?   No, not all students are good at learning languages; some are good at learning languages and some are bad at learning languages

98   ## instead of

Do you prefer tea instead of coffee?   Yes, I prefer tea instead of coffee ~ No, I don't prefer tea instead of coffee; I prefer coffee instead of tea

Do you prefer coming to school instead of going to the cinema?   No, I don't prefer coming to school instead of going to the cinema; I prefer going to the cinema instead of coming to school

Do you prefer walking instead of going by car?   Yes, I prefer walking instead of going by car ~ No, I don't prefer walking instead of going by car; I prefer going by car instead of walking

 *Dictation 6*

We're reading,/ not writing./ That's his pullover/ and these are/ her tights./ These are/ our skirts./ Those are/ their trousers./ Your handkerchief/ is in/ your pocket./ Her blouse is grey./ Miss Smith/ is not French/ or German;/ she's English./ Give me/ the last match/ in your hand./ We say/ one person,/ but two people./ He's coming from London/ and going to Beijing./ This is my finger,/ not my thumb.

 *Do Revision Exercise 3*

LESSON 19

99   bread   butter   rice

What do we put on our bread?   We put butter on our bread

Do you like bread without butter?   Yes, I like bread without butter ~ No, I don't like bread without butter; I only like bread with butter

What colour's butter?   Butter's yellow or white

Do you prefer white or brown rice?   I prefer ... rice

carry

What am I doing?   You're carrying your chair to the window

Do you think you can carry this table on your back?   Yes, I think I can carry this table on my back ~ No, I don't think I can carry this table on my back

Am I carrying a tie (or dress etc.)?   No, you aren't carrying a tie; you're wearing a tie

Am I wearing a handkerchief?   No, you aren't wearing a handkerchief; you're carrying a handkerchief

100   no = not any

The word "no" can mean "not any". For example, we can say "I have <u>not</u> got <u>any</u> books" or "I have got <u>no</u> books"; the sentences have the same meaning.

What can we say instead of "not any books"?   We can say "no books" instead of "not any books"

Give me another example, please.   "They haven't got any friends" or "They have no friends"

hear

Can you hear me speaking to you? — Yes, I can hear you speaking to me

Can you hear anybody in the other room? — Yes, I can hear somebody in the other room ~ No, I can't hear anybody in the other room

What do we hear with? — We hear with our ears

drive

Can you drive a car? — Yes, I can drive a car ~ No, I can't drive a car

Is there anybody in your family who can't drive a car? — Yes, there's somebody in my family who can't drive a car ~ No, there isn't anybody in my family who can't drive a car

money pence pound

How much money have you got in your pocket (or bag)? — I've got about ... in my pocket (or bag)

How many pence make a pound? — A hundred pence make a pound

How many euros (or dollars etc.) make a pound? — About ... euros (or dollars etc.) make a pound

fewer ... than

Have I got more thumbs than fingers on my hands? — No, you haven't got more thumbs than fingers on your hands; you've got fewer thumbs than fingers on your hands

Are there more pages in this book than in that book? — No, there aren't more pages in this book than in that book; there are fewer pages in this book than in that book

Are there more people in Europe than in Asia? — No, there aren't more people in Europe than in Asia; there are fewer people in Europe than in Asia

Are there more tables in this school than chairs? — No, there aren't more tables in this school than chairs; there are fewer tables in this school than chairs

watch

What's the difference between a watch and a clock? The difference between a watch and a clock is that we wear a watch on our wrist, whereas we hang a clock on the wall or put it on a table

What's the difference between "wear" and "carry"? The difference between "wear" and "carry" is that we use "wear" for a thing that is on the body, whereas we use "carry" for a thing that is not on the body

Is there a clock in this room? Yes, there's a clock in this room ~ No, there isn't a clock in this room

Am I carrying a watch? No, you aren't carrying a watch; you're wearing a watch

What are you carrying in your pocket (or bag)? I'm carrying ... in my pocket (or bag)

LESSON 20

103   *See Chart 6*

time   past   to   by   o'clock

What's the time by this clock?   It's 3 o'clock etc.

What's the time now, please?   It's ... now

With the numbers 5, 10, 20, and 25 we don't say "minutes". For example, we say "It's 5 past 3." With the numbers between one and five, five and ten etc. we say "minutes". For example, "It's 2 minutes past 4."

day   week   month   year

How many seconds make a minute?   60 seconds make a minute

How many minutes make an hour?   60 minutes make an hour

How many hours make a day?   24 hours make a day

How many days make a week?   7 days make a week

How many weeks make a month?   4 weeks make a month

How many months make a year?   12 months make a year

104   **also**

Give me an example of the word "also", please.   I can speak my language and I can also speak English

meat   sugar

Do you like meat?   Yes, I like meat ~ No, I don't like meat

What colour's sugar?   Sugar's white or brown

Do you put sugar on your meat?	No, I don't put sugar on my meat; I put it in my tea or coffee

count   from ... to

1, 2, 3, 4, 5 – What am I doing?	You're counting
6, 7, 8, 9, 10 – What am I doing?	You're counting the numbers from six to ten
Count the numbers from 100 to 105, please.	One hundred, one hundred and one, one hundred and two ...
What's he/she doing?	He/She's counting the numbers from 100 to 105

Possessive adjectives	Possessive pronouns
my	mine
your	yours
his	his
her	hers
its	-
our	ours
your	yours
their	theirs

What are the possessive adjectives?	The possessive adjectives are "my", "your" ...
What are the possessive pronouns?	The possessive pronouns are "mine", "yours" ...

The difference between a possessive adjective and a possessive pronoun is that we put a possessive adjective in front of a noun (for example, "This is my book"), whereas we use a possessive pronoun instead of a noun. For example, instead of saying "This is my pen and that is her pen", we can say "This is my pen and that is hers".

What's the difference between a possessive adjective and a possessive pronoun?

The difference between a possessive adjective and a possessive pronoun is that we put a possessive adjective in front of a noun whereas we use a possessive pronoun instead of a noun

106 Give me an example, please.

This is my book. This book is mine. This is mine.

mine	**yours**
Is this your ear?	No, that isn't my ear; it's your ear
Is this ear yours?	No, that ear isn't mine; it's yours
Is that nose mine?	No, this nose isn't yours; it's mine

See Chart 1

his	**hers**
Is that dress his?	No, that dress isn't his; it's hers
Is that suit hers?	No, that suit isn't hers; it's his
Are those hands his?	No, those hands aren't his; they're hers
Are those arms hers?	No, those arms aren't hers; they're his

ours	**theirs**
Are those legs ours?	No, those legs aren't ours; they're theirs
Are these their books?	No, these aren't their books; they're our books

107 Are these books theirs?   No, these books aren't theirs; they're ours

Infinitive

Verbs in the infinitive generally have the word "to" in front of them. For example, "to do", "to come", "to go" etc.

Give me some examples of verbs in the infinitive, please.
> Some examples of verbs in the infinitive are "to come", "to go", "to take" etc.

Auxiliary verb   do

An auxiliary verb is part of the verb in a sentence, but it does not tell us the action. For example, in the sentence "We are speaking", the word "speaking" tells us the action, and the word "are" is an auxiliary verb. In the sentence "He can read", the word "can" is the auxiliary verb. The auxiliary verb for the present simple is "do". For example, we say "<u>Do</u> you speak English?" or "I <u>do</u> not have a bag".

Which word is the auxiliary verb in this sentence: "They can open the window"?
> The word "can" is the auxiliary verb in that sentence

Which word is the auxiliary verb in this sentence: "Do they walk to school?"
> The word "do" is the auxiliary verb in that sentence

Also, the word "do" means (translate into student's language). **For example, "What is he doing?" – "He's sitting on a chair".**

What does the verb "to do" mean?	The verb "to do" means ...
What am I doing?	You're going out of the room
What do I do after the lesson?	You go out of the room after the lesson
What am I doing?	You're sitting down
What do you do before the lesson?	I sit down before the lesson
What am I doing?	You're standing up
What do you do after the lesson?	I stand up after the lesson

 *Dictation 7*

This part of the body/ is a leg/ and this/ is an arm./ The plural of "foot"/ is "feet"./ There are twelve words/ in this sentence./ A verb is a word/ we use for an action./ What does the word/ "do" mean?/ As an auxiliary verb/ it means nothing./ We say "the book",/ but "the umbrella"./ Question mark, full stop,/ comma./ The letter A/ isn't a consonant,/ but a vowel./ This answer is wrong./ That is right.

LESSON 21

109 **the most**

Of these three books, which book has the most pages?   Of these three books, this book has the most pages

Which city in this country has the most people?   ... is the city in this country which has the most people

Which person in your family reads the most books?   My ... is the person in my family who reads the most books

Which school in this town has the most students?   ... is the school in this town which has the most students

beautiful   **handsome**   **ugly**

Do you think Paris is an ugly city?   No, I don't think Paris is an ugly city; I think it's a beautiful city

Do you think ... is a beautiful place?   No, I don't think ... is a beautiful place; I think it's an ugly place

Do you think (use here the name of a film star) **is ugly?**   No, I don't think ... is ugly; I think she's beautiful/he's handsome

110 Which do you think's the most beautiful place in this country?   I think ... is the most beautiful place in this country

eat

What am I doing?   You're eating

Do you eat all food?   No, I don't eat all food; some I eat and some I don't eat

Do you eat bread without butter?   Yes, I eat bread without butter ~ No, I don't eat bread without butter

What do we eat with?   We eat with our mouths

drink   water   wine   milk

What am I doing?	You're drinking
Do you drink tea?	Yes, I drink tea ~ No, I don't drink tea
Can we drink meat?	No, we can't drink meat; we eat meat
Tell me the names of some drinks, please.	The names of some drinks are water, wine and milk
What colour's water?	Water has no colour
Is there a drink on the table?	Yes there's a drink on the table ~ No, there isn't a drink on the table
Do you drink wine?	Yes, I drink wine ~ No, I don't drink wine
Which drink do you prefer: milk or water?	I prefer ...

metal   gold   silver   steel   iron

Tell me the names of four metals, please.	The names of four metals are gold, silver, steel and iron

made of   key   plastic

Is your watch made of plastic?	Yes, my watch is made of plastic ~ No, my watch isn't made of plastic; it's made of ...
What's a key generally made of?	A key's generally made of steel
Are you wearing anything made of silver?	Yes, I'm wearing something made of silver ~ No, I'm not wearing anything made of silver

cost

How much do you think this pen costs?	I think that pen costs about ...
Do your shoes cost more than your handkerchief?	Yes, my shoes cost more than my handkerchief
How much does the cinema cost in this town?	The cinema costs about ... in this town

like

What does the word "like" mean (not the verb)? The word "like" means "similar to" or "such as"

Is this book like that book? Yes, this book is like that book

Is your face the same as your father's? No, my face isn't the same as my father's; it's like my father's

Do you eat different kinds of food, like Chinese, Indian, Spanish etc.? Yes, I eat different kinds of food, like Chinese, Indian, Spanish etc. ~ No, I don't eat different kinds of food, like Chinese, Indian, Spanish etc.

Monday	**Tuesday**	**Wednesday**
Thursday	**Friday**	**Saturday**
Sunday	**weekend**	

113 Tell me the names of the days of the week, please. The names of the days of the week are Monday, Tuesday, Wednesday, Thursday, Friday, Saturday and Sunday

What do we call Saturday and Sunday? We call Saturday and Sunday the weekend

today	**yesterday**	**tomorrow**
was	**will be**	**to be**

What's today? Today's ...

What was yesterday? Yesterday was ...

What will tomorrow be? Tomorrow will be ...

What will the day after tomorrow be? The day after tomorrow will be ...

What was the day before yesterday? The day before yesterday was ...

LESSON 22

114 **want**   **at the moment**

Do you want to break your pen?   No, I don't want to break my pen

Do you want to break the window?   No, I don't want to break the window

Do you want anything to eat at the moment?   Yes, I want something to eat at the moment ~ No, I don't want anything to eat at the moment

Do you want anything to drink at the moment?   Yes, I want something to drink at the moment ~ No, I don't want anything to drink at the moment

do you have ...?   **you don't have ...**

Instead of using "got" with the verb "have", we can use the present simple auxiliary "do". We can say "Have you got a pen?" or "Do you have a pen?" We can say "You haven't got any money" or "You don't have any money". There is no difference.

Do you have anything in your pocket (or bag)?   Yes, I have something in my pocket (or bag)

What do they have on their feet?   They have shoes on their feet

Do you have any relatives in this town?   Yes, I have some relatives in this town ~ No, I don't have any relatives in this town

115 **begin**   **end**   **last**   **how long**

At what time does the lesson begin?   The lesson begins at ...

At what time does the lesson end?   The lesson ends at ...

How long does the lesson last?   The lesson lasts ...

cheap   expensive   Rolls Royce

Is this pen expensive?   No, that pen isn't expensive; it's cheap

Is a Rolls Royce cheap?   No, a Rolls Royce isn't cheap; it's expensive

Is my handkerchief expensive?   No, your handkerchief isn't expensive; it's cheap

the fewest

Of these three books, has this book got the most pages?   No, of these three books, that book hasn't got the most pages; it's got the fewest pages

Which person in your family reads the fewest books?   My ... is the person in my family who reads the fewest books

Of these three countries, Germany, France, and Greece, has Greece got the most people?   No, of those three countries, Greece hasn't got the most people; it's got the fewest people

building

About how many rooms are there in this building?   There are about ... rooms in this building

Is this building high (or low)?   No, this building isn't ... ; it's ...

inside   outside   stomach

What part of the box is this?   It's the inside of the box

What part of the box is this?   It's the outside of the box

What can you see outside this window?   I can see a building etc. outside this window

Are we sitting outside in the corridor?   No, we aren't sitting outside in the corridor; we're sitting inside the classroom

Is there any food inside our stomachs after eating?   Yes, there's some food inside our stomachs after eating

117 **a**   **some**

The plural of "a" is "some". For example, we say "a pen", but "some pens".

What's the plural of "a"?	The plural of "a" is "some"
What's the plural of "a book"?	The plural of "a book" is "some books"
What can you see in this classroom?	I can see some books, some pens, a teacher, a door etc. in this classroom
Have I got a thumb on my left hand?	Yes, you've got a thumb on your left hand
Have I got any fingers on my left hand?	Yes, you've got some fingers on your left hand

well

Can you hear well?	Yes, I can hear well
Can you see well?	Yes, I can see well
Can you speak ... well?	Yes, I can speak ... well

flower   plant

Do you like the smell of flowers?	Yes, I like the smell of flowers
Have you got any plants at home?	Yes, I've got some plants at home ~ No, I haven't got any plants at home

118 **whose**

Whose book's this?	It's your book
Whose hand's that?	It's his/her hand
Whose suit's that?	It's Mr Brown's suit

love	hate
Do children generally love going to school?	No, children don't generally love going to school; they generally hate going to school
Do children hate their mothers?	No, children don't hate their mothers; they love their mothers
Do you love eating bad food?	No, I don't love eating bad food; I hate eating bad food
Do you hate all food?	No, I don't hate all food; some I hate and some I love

 *Dictation 8*

What is the meaning/ of the word "wrist"?/ How many things/ are there here?/ Her hair/ is on her head./ His chin,/ mouth and nose/ are on his face./ My eyes are blue./ The people of Scandinavia/ are tall./ He's asking us a question./ The name of her country/ is Germany./ Who are you?/ The contraction/ of the verb "to have"/ is "I've, you've, he's" etc./ Have you got any ears?/ Yes, two.

 *Do Revision Exercise 4*

LESSON 23

119 **meal**   **breakfast**   **lunch**

dinner   **a day**   **morning**   **evening**

Tell me the names of the three meals that people generally eat a day.
    The names of the three meals that people generally eat a day are breakfast, lunch and dinner

What time do you have your breakfast?   I have my breakfast at …

What time do you have your lunch?   I have my lunch at …

What time does your dinner begin?   My dinner begins at …

What time does your dinner end?   My dinner ends at …

How long does his/her dinner last?   His/her dinner lasts …

plate   **bowl**   **knife**   **fork**

spoon   **chopsticks**

120 What do we eat our food from?   We eat our food from a plate or a bowl

What do we eat our food with?   We eat our food with a knife, fork and spoon, or with chopsticks

See Chart 7

many	more … than	the most
few	fewer … than	the fewest
much	more … than	the most
little	less … than	the least

exception**quantity****singular**

"Many" and "much" have the same meaning, but we use "many" with things we can count. For example, we can count pens – one pen, two pens, three pens etc. We can count books, chairs etc. Generally, the things we can count have an "s" in the plural. "People" is an exception. It has no "s", but it is plural and we use "many" with it. For example, "There are many people in this town".

We use "much" with things we cannot count. For example, we cannot count water or sugar. We cannot say "one water, two waters"; "one sugar, two sugars" etc. These things are a singular quantity and have no "s". Money is not an exception; we can count money, but we do not say "one money, two monies". We say "one pound, two pounds"; "one dollar, two dollars" etc.

What's the difference between "many" and "much"?   The difference between "many" and "much" is that we use "many" with things we can count, and "much" with things we can't count

121 Give me a sentence with "many" in it, please.   There are many cars in a large city

Give me a sentence with "much" in it.   I do not put much sugar in my tea

"Few" and "little" also have the same meaning, but we use "few" with things we can count, and "little" with things we cannot count.

What's the difference between "few" and "little"?   The difference between "few" and "little" is that we use "few" with things we can count and "little" with things we can't count

Give me a sentence with "few" in it, please.   There are few tables in this school

Give me a sentence with "little" in it.   I drink little milk

many	**few**
Are there many pictures on these walls?	No, there aren't many pictures on these walls; there are few pictures on these walls
Are there few people in a large city?	No, there aren't few people in a large city; there are many people in a large city

much   **little**   **a lot of**

salt   **pepper**

We can use "much" in questions and negative sentences, but in positive sentences we generally use "a lot of". For example, we do not say "I eat much bread"; we say "I eat a lot of bread".

Do you drink much water?	Yes, I drink <u>a lot of</u> water
Do you drink little water?	No, I don't drink little water; I drink a lot of water
Do you eat little bread?	No, I don't eat little bread; I eat a lot of bread
Do you eat much salt?	No, I don't eat much salt; I eat little salt
Do you put much pepper on your plate?	No, I don't put much pepper on my plate; I put little pepper on my plate

fewer ... than   **less ... than**   **bank**

The difference between "fewer ... than" and "less ... than" is that we use "fewer ... than" with things we can count, and "less ... than" with things we cannot count. For example, "I have <u>fewer</u> thumbs than fingers. I drink <u>less</u> milk than water".

What's the difference between "fewer ... than" and "less ... than"?
    The difference between "fewer ... than" and "less ... than" is that we use "fewer ... than" with things we can count, and "less ... than" with things we can't count

Give me a sentence with "fewer ... than" in it, please. There are fewer pictures in this room than chairs

Give me a sentence with "less ... than" in it. I eat less food than my brother

Are there more people in Europe than in Asia? No, there aren't more people in Europe than in Asia; there are fewer people in Europe than in Asia

Do you drink more milk than water? No, I don't drink more milk than water; I drink less milk than water

123 Have you got more money than the bank of England? No, I haven't got more money than the Bank of England; I've got less money than the Bank of England

Do you eat more meat than bread? No, I don't eat more meat than bread; I eat less meat than bread

LESSON 24

124 **the fewest**   **the least**   **the one**

The difference between "the fewest" and "the least" is the same as the difference between "fewer ... than" and "less ... than". We use "the fewest" with things we can count, whereas we use "the least" we use with things we cannot count. For example, "Of these three places, London, Cambridge and Greenwich, Greenwich has <u>the fewest buildings</u>", and "Of these three people, Mr Brown, Mr Smith and Mr Jones, Mr Jones drinks <u>the least coffee</u>".

What's the difference between "the fewest" and "the least"?
> The difference between "the fewest" and "the least" is that we use "the fewest" with things we can count, whereas we use "the least" with things we can't count

Give me a sentence with "the fewest" in it, please.
> In my family, my brother is the one who reads the fewest books

Give me a sentence with "the least" in it.
> In my family, my sister is the one who eats the least bread

Of these three books, has this book got the most pages?
> No, of these three books, this book hasn't got the most pages; it's got the fewest pages

Who eats the least food in your family?
> My ... eats the least food in my family

Who drinks the least coffee in your family?
> My ... drinks the least coffee in my family

125 Of these three foods, bread, meat and salt, do you eat salt the most?
> No, of those three foods, bread, meat and salt, I don't eat salt the most; I eat it the least

Of these three drinks, water, milk and wine, do you drink wine the most?
> No, of those three drinks, water, milk and wine, I don't drink wine the most; I drink it the least

opposite   next to

Who's sitting opposite you?   ... is sitting opposite me

Who's sitting next to you?   ... is sitting next to me

What can you see opposite this building?   I can see another
                                                                                    building etc. opposite this building

work   rest   most people

Do most people rest from Monday to Friday?   No, most people don't
                                                                              rest from Monday to Friday; they work

Do you think most people like working?   No, I don't think
                                                                                        most people like working;
                                                                                        I think they dislike working

Do you work at the weekend?   Yes, I work at the weekend
                                                                                 ~ No, I don't work at the weekend

glass   wood

What's the window made of?   The window's made of glass

Is the table made of plastic?   No, the table isn't made of plastic;
                                                                                                  it's made of wood

paper   stone

What's this book made of?   This (or that) book's made of paper

What's the wall of the house behind Mr and Mrs Brown made of?
                                                                                         The wall of the house behind
                                                                                       Mr and Mrs Brown is made of stone

enough

Do you speak English well?   No, I don't speak English well,
                                                                                        but I speak it well enough

Are you tall enough to touch the ceiling?   No, I'm not tall enough
                                                                                 to touch the ceiling; I'm too short

Are you short enough to stand under the table?   No, I'm not short
                                                                                 enough to stand under the table; I'm too tall

127   Is my pocket large enough to put this book into?   No, your pocket isn't large enough to put that book into; it's too small

 *See Chart 1*

that one   repeat

Instead of saying "This pencil is black and that pencil is white", we can say "This pencil is black and that <u>one</u> is white", without repeating the word "pencil".

What colour's this pencil?	This pencil's black
What colour's that one?	That one's white
Which pencil's red?	This pencil's red
Which one's grey?	This one's grey
Which book's open?	This book's open
Which one's closed?	This one's closed

badly

Can you hear well with your fingers in your ears?	No, I can't hear well with my fingers in my ears; I hear badly
Do you see badly?	Yes, I see badly ~ No, I don't see badly; I see well
128 Does this pen write badly?	No, this pen doesn't write badly; it writes well
Do you speak ... badly?	No, I don't speak ... badly; I speak it well

telephone	mobile	phone
call	make a (phone) call	

Is there a telephone in your family home? Yes, there's a telephone in my family home ~ No, there isn't a telephone in my family home

Have you got a mobile (phone) in your pocket? Yes, I've got a mobile (phone) in my pocket ~ No, I haven't got a mobile (phone) in my pocket

How many phone calls do you make a day? I make about ... phone calls a day

Dictation 9

The difference/ between "any" and "some"/ is that we generally use "any"/ in questions and negative sentences,/ whereas we use "some"/ in the positive./ "Any" is non-specific./ "How many" is specific./ Are there any books/ on the table?/ Yes, there are some./ How many books are there/ on the floor?/ There are none./ The present continuous/ we use for an action/ we are doing now./ For example,/ I am speaking English now./ About how many pages/ are there in this book?

Do Revision Exercise 5

Pronunciation Chart

/ɪ/		/əʊ/		/ɜː/		/ʌ/	
this	/ðɪs/	no	/nəʊ/	first	/fɜːst/	front	/frʌnt/
it's	/ɪts/	coat	/kəʊt/	third	/θɜːd/	London	/ˈlʌndən/
is	/ɪz/	don't	/dəʊnt/	her	/hɜː/	coming	/kʌmɪŋ/
city	/ˈsɪti/	both	/bəʊθ/	person	/ˈpɜːsən/	country	/ˈkʌntri/
miss	/mɪs/	only	/ˈəʊnli/	word	/wɜːd/	mother	/ˈmʌðə/
in	/ɪn/	most	/məʊst/	verb	/vɜːb/	some	/sʌm/
difference	/ˈdɪfrəns/	home	/həʊm/	prefer	/prəˈfɜː/	son	/sʌn/
still	/stɪl/			turn	/tɜːn/	money	/ˈmʌni/
difficult	/ˈdɪfɪkəlt/					month	/mʌnθ/
milk	/mɪlk/					love	/lʌv/
little	/ˈlɪtl/						

Pronunciation Chart

/æ/		/ɔ:/		/ʊ/		/h/		other	
as	/æz/	all	/ɔ:l/	look	/lʊk/	home	/həʊm/	a	/ə/
hat	/hæt/	more	/mɔ:/	book	/bʊk/	hat	/hæt/	an	/æn/
have	/hæv/	door	/dɔ:/			head	/hed/	what	/wɒt/
man	/mæn/	wall	/wɔ:l/			hear	/hɪə/	the book	/ðə/
		call	/kɔ:l/			her	/hɜ:/	the eye	/ði:/
								we're	/wɪə/
								answering	/ˈɑ:nsərɪŋ/
								or	/ɔ:/
								fifth	/fɪfθ/

1) This is his city.

2) Oh, no; don't go home.

3) The third, thirteenth and thirty-third.

4) Send some money to London.

5) Have you got that hat?

6) There are doors in all the walls.

7) Look at the book.

8) Her hat is on his head.

Revision Exercise 2 (Lessons 6 – 9)

1. Is India in Europe?
2. What are the cardinal numbers?
3. What are the ordinal numbers?
4. Which's the first letter of the alphabet?
5. Which's the twelfth letter of the alphabet?
6. Which's the last letter of the alphabet?
7. Are all the walls in this room white?
8. What's the plural of person?
9. What's the plural of foot?
10. 2 + 2 = 7: is that right?
11. What's your name?
12. Are you going to the window?
13. What's the name of your country?
14. What's the name of the country between England and Spain?
15. Are the people of Scandinavia short?
16. What's the difference between "tall" and "short" and "high" and "low"?
17. What's the difference between "any" and "some"?
18. Are there any chairs on the table?
19. How many books are there on the table?
20. How many books are there on the floor?

Answers

1. No, India isn't in Europe; it's in Asia.
2. The cardinal numbers are 1, 2, 3 etc.
3. The ordinal numbers are 1st, 2nd, 3rd etc.
4. A's the first letter of the alphabet.
5. L's the twelfth letter of the alphabet.
6. Z's the last letter of the alphabet.

7   Yes, all the walls in this room are white.
8   The plural of person is people.
9   The plural of foot is feet.
10 No, it isn't right; it's wrong.
11 My name's ...
12 No, I'm not going to the window; I'm remaining on the chair.
13 ... is the name of my country.
14 France's the name of the country between England and Spain.
15 No, the people of Scandinavia aren't short; they're tall.
16 The difference between "tall" and "short" and "high" and "low" is that we use "tall" and "short" for people, whereas we use "high" and "low" for things.
17 The difference between "any" and "some" is that we use "any" in questions and negative sentences, whereas we use "some" in positive sentences.
18 No, there aren't any chairs on the table.
19 There are ... books on the table.
20 There are none.

Revision Exercise 3 (Lessons 10 – 11)

1   Are you speaking?
2   What's the difference between the present continuous and the present simple?
3   Are you writing?
4   Do you write?
5   What's the negative of "I speak"?
6   What's the negative of "he speaks"?
7   About how many people are there in your country?
8   Can you read and write?
9   Do you like your city (or town or village)?
10 Do you dislike television?

11 Are all the parts of your body still now?
12 What clothes are you wearing?
13 Are you wearing glasses?
14 Do you wear a hat?
15 Do we speak with our mouths?
16 Do we read with our eyes?
17 How much is half a hundred?
18 How much is half thirteen?
19 Tell me your name, please.
20 Tell me the name of the capital of Russia, please.

Answers

1 No, I'm not speaking, I'm reading.
2 The difference between the present continuous and the present simple is that we use the present continuous for an action we are doing now, whereas we use the present simple for an action we do generally.
3 Yes, I'm writing.
4 Yes, I write.
5 The negative of "I speak" is "I don't speak".
6 The negative of "he speaks" is "he doesn't speak".
7 There are about ... people in my country.
8 Yes, I can read and write.
9 Yes, I like my city (or town or village). ~ No, I don't like my city (or town or village).
10 No, I don't dislike television; I like television.
11 No, not all the parts of my body are still now; my mouth and my tongue etc. are moving.
12 I'm wearing shoes, socks, a suit, etc.
13 Yes, I'm wearing glasses. ~ No, I'm not wearing glasses.
14 Yes, I wear a hat.
15 Yes, we speak with our mouths.

16 Yes, we read with our eyes.

17 Fifty is half a hundred.

18 Six and a half is half thirteen.

19 My name's ...

20 Moscow's the capital of Russia.

Revision Exercise 4 (Lessons 12 – 13)

1   Do you speak (Greek)?

2   Which do you prefer: the cinema or television?

3   Do the English generally prefer coffee?

4   Which is it right to say: "both us" or "both of us?

5   Which language do you generally speak?

6   Is Germany an Asian country?

7   What's the contraction of "I have not"?

8   Have you got two heads?

9   Are the French the same as the Russians?

10 Do the people in Germany speak the same language as the people in Japan?

11 Which is it right to say, "people are" or "people is"?

12 What's the difference between "anybody" and "somebody"?

13 Is there anybody speaking to you?

14 Do you like walking?

15 Do you sit down after the lesson?

16 What's the negative of "can"?

17 Can you touch the ceiling?

18 How much is a quarter of a thousand?

19 What's a quarter of five?

20 Do you like learning a language?

Answers

1. No, I don't speak (Greek); I speak ...
2. I prefer... to...
3. No, the English don't generally prefer coffee; they generally prefer tea.
4. It's right to say "both of us".
5. I generally speak ...
6. No, Germany isn't an Asian country; it's a European country.
7. The contraction of "I have not" is "I haven't".
8. No, I haven't got two heads; I've only got one head.
9. No, the French aren't the same as the Russians; they're different from the Russians.
10. No, the people in Germany don't speak the same language as the people in Japan; they speak a different language from the people in Japan.
11. It's right to say "people are".
12. The difference between "anybody" and "somebody" is that we use "anybody" in questions and negative sentences, whereas we use "somebody" in positive sentences.
13. No, there isn't anybody speaking to me.
14. Yes, I like walking.
15. No, I don't sit down after the lesson; I stand up after the lesson.
16. The negative of "can" is "cannot".
17. No, I can't touch the ceiling.
18. 250 is a quarter of a thousand.
19. One-and-a-quarter is a quarter of five.
20. Yes, I like learning a language.

Revision Exercise 5 (Lessons 14 – 15)

1. Is Chinese an easy language to learn?
2. Do you come to school by train or by bus?
3. Are you married?

4   How many children have your mother and father got?
5   What do we call the thing we wear on our heads?
6   What kind of room is this?
7   Give me some examples of prepositions, please.
8   What do we speak with?
9   Tell me the names of the four cardinal points, please.
10 Is Greece west of Italy?
11 Is Paris in the south of France?
12 Tell me the names of some of the places you like in this country.
13 What's the opposite of "high"?
14 Can we speak without opening our mouths?
15 Can you read without wearing glasses?
16 What's the difference between a verb and a noun?
17 Give me an example of a verb, please.
18 Give me an example of a noun.
19 Is the word "translation" a verb or a noun?
20 Do you walk about the room during the lesson?

Answers
1   No, Chinese isn't an easy language to learn; it's a difficult language to learn.
2   I come to school by …
3   Yes, I'm married. ~ No, I'm not married; I'm single.
4   My mother and father have got … children.
5   We call the thing we wear on our heads a hat.
6   It's a classroom.
7   Some examples of prepositions are "on", "under", "in" and "from".
8   We speak with our mouths.
9   The names of the four cardinal points are north, south, east and west.
10 No, Greece isn't west of Italy; it's east of Italy.
11 No, Paris isn't in the south of France; it's in the north of France.

12. The names of some of the places I like in this country are …
13. The opposite of "high" is "low".
14. No, we can't speak without opening our mouths.
15. Yes, I can read without wearing glasses. ~ No, I can't read without wearing glasses.
16. The difference between a verb and a noun is that a verb is a word we use for an action, whereas a noun is the name of a thing.
17. "Take" is a verb.
18. "Book" is a noun.
19. The word "translation" is a noun.
20. No, I don't walk about the room during the lesson; I sit on my chair.

Demonstration Charts

Chart 1

Chart 1

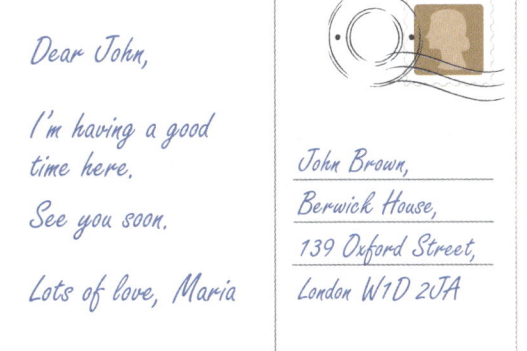

Chart 4

non-specific	Any?
specific	How many?
non-specific	Anybody?
specific	Who?
non-specific	Anything?
specific	What?

Yes, some
No, not any

Seven etc.
None

Yes, somebody
No, not anybody

Mrs Brown etc.
Nobody

Yes, something
No, not anything

A light etc.
Nothing

Present continuous – now

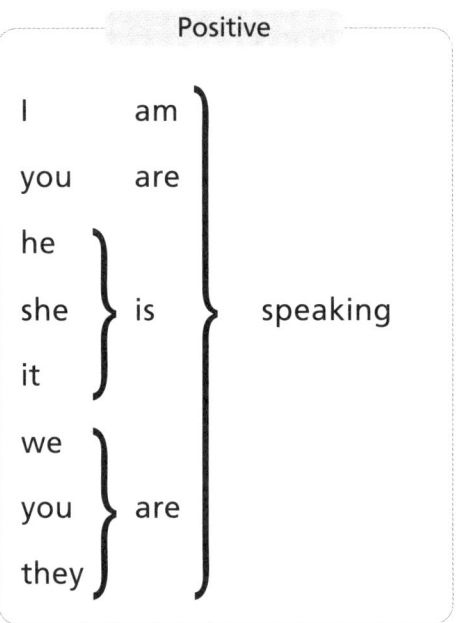

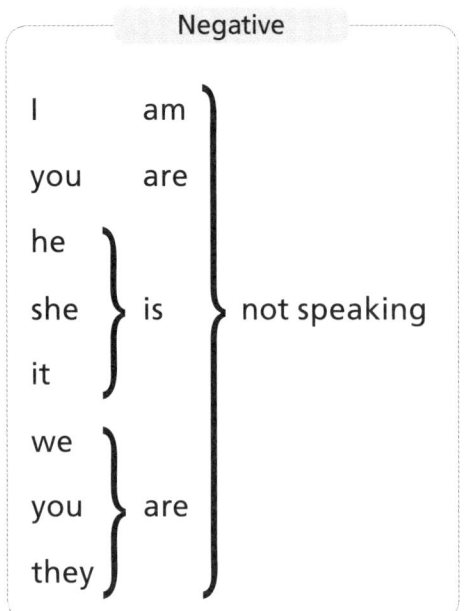

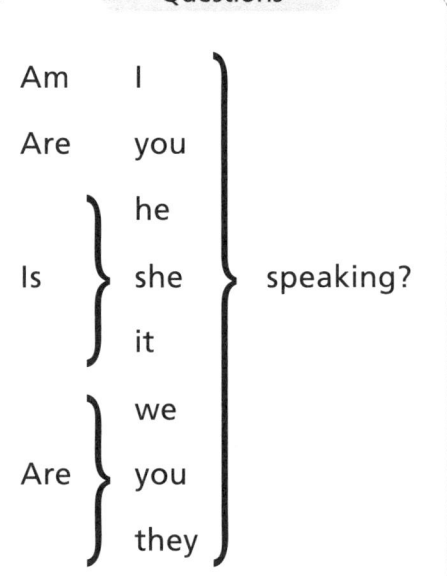

Present simple – generally

Positive

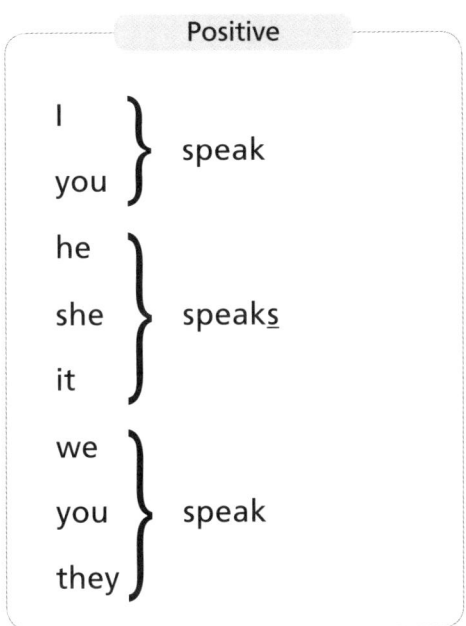

Negative

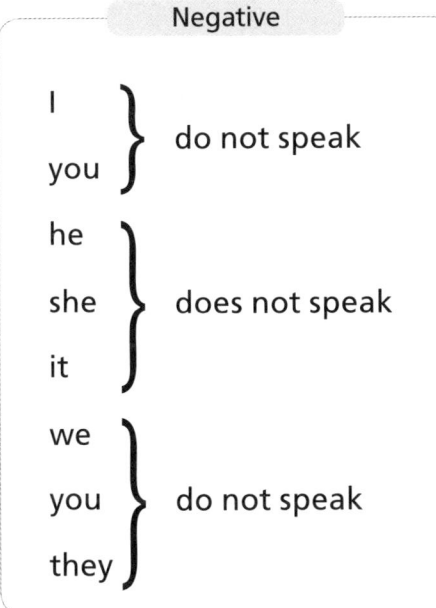

Questions

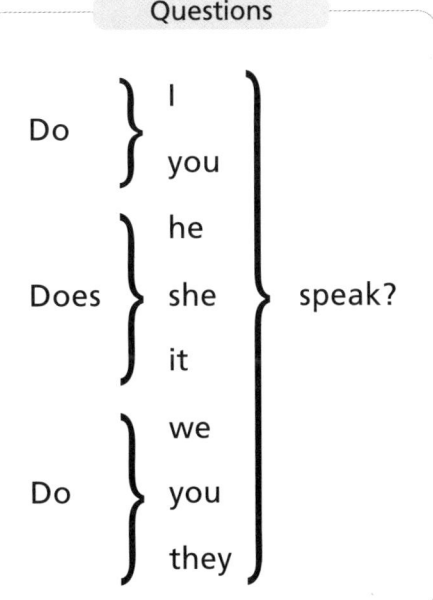

Chart 6

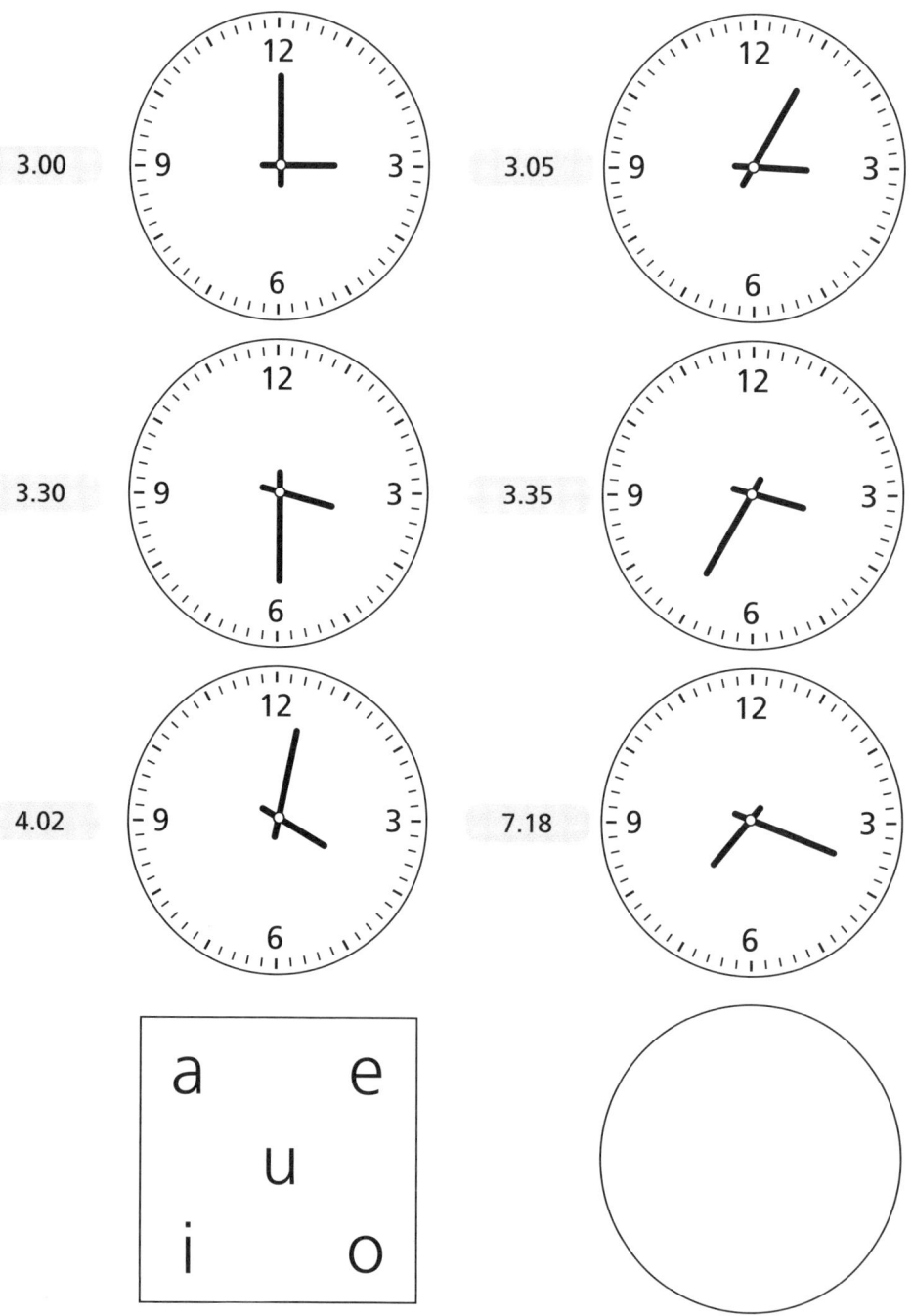

Chart 6

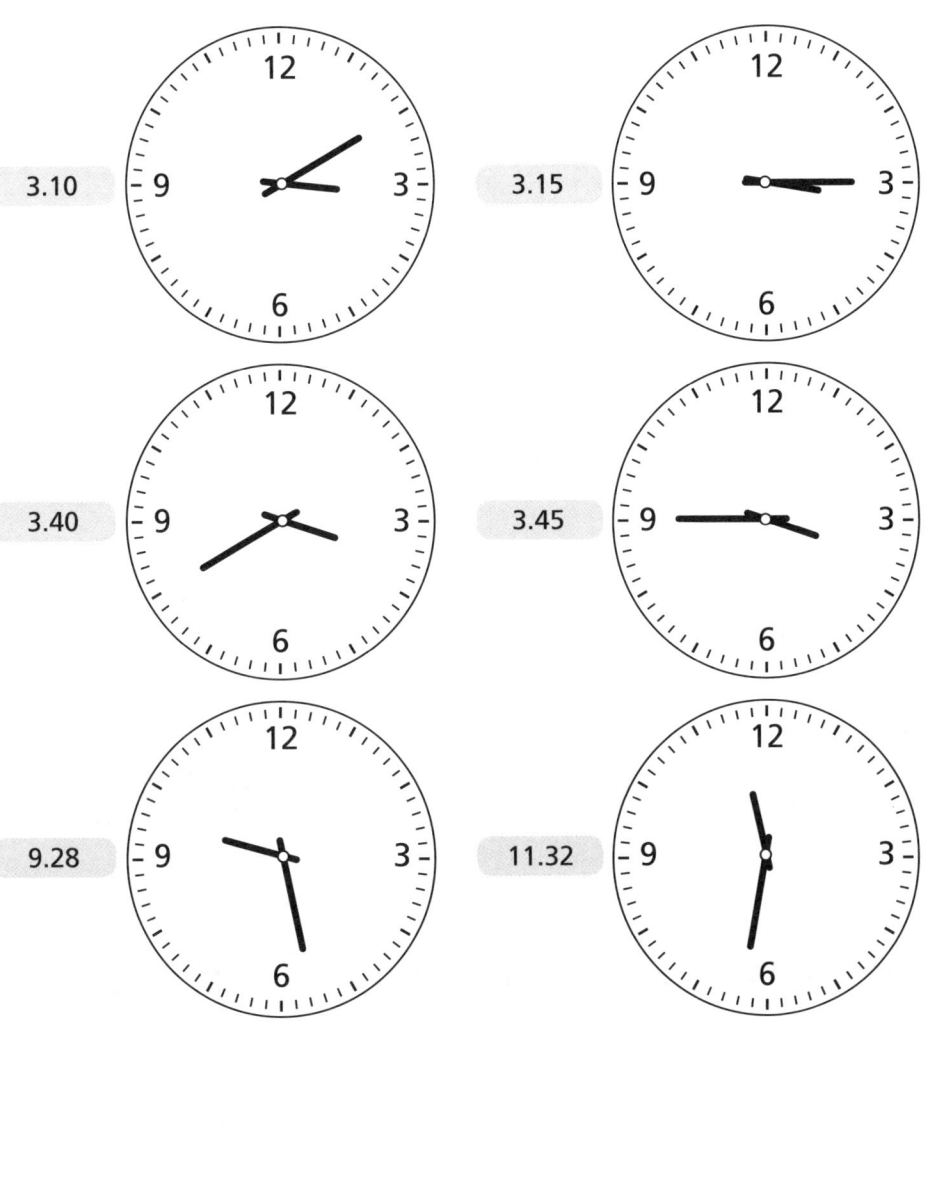

Chart 7

PLURAL — NUMBER —

many   —   more ... than   —

few   —   fewer ... than   —

SINGULAR — QUANTITY —

much   —   more ... than   —

little   —   less ... than   —

THINGS WE CAN COUNT

the most   books

                pens

the fewest   people

THINGS WE CAN'T COUNT

the most   water

                sugar

the least   money

Index

a 117
a day 119
a lot of 121
about 62
about 84
address 89
adjective 93
also 104
another 91
anybody 71
anything 85
Asian 68
at the moment 114
aunt 95
auxiliary verb 107
back 88
bad 97
bad at 97
badly 127
bank 122
beautiful 109
because 92
begin 115
both 66
bottom 88
bowl 119
bread 99
break 96
breakfast 119
brother 94
building 116
bus 77
butter 99
by 77, 103
call 78, 128
can 62
cannot / can't 74
car 77
cardinal point 82
carry 99
cheap 115
child 78
children 78
Chinese 56
chopsticks 119
cinema 62
coffee 66
completely 63
corridor 72
cost 112
count 104
cousin 95
dad 78
daughter 94

day 103
different ... from 69
difficult 76
dinner 119
dislike 62
do 56, 107
do not 58
do you have ...? 114
does 56
does not 58
doesn't 58
don't 58
down 74
drink 110
drive 100
during 84
east 82
easy 76
eat 110
end 115
enough 126
European 68
evening 119
exception 120
expensive 115
family 95
father 78
few 90, 121
fewer ... than ... 101,122
flower 117
food 94
fork 119
Friday 112
friend 90
friendly 90
from .... to 104
front 88
Germany 68
glass 126
glasses 64
gold 111
good 97
good at 97
goodbye 67
grammar 76
Greek 66
Greenwich 92
half 65
handsome 109
hang 76
hate 118
he has not /
he hasn't 68
hear 100

hello 67
hers 106
his 106
home 53
hour 92
how long 115
husband 77
I have not /
I haven't 68
in 91
infinitive 107
inside 116
instead of 98
into 91
iron 111
it has not / it hasn't .. 68
Japan 69
Japanese 56
key 111
kind 79
knife 119
language 68
last 115
learn 75
left 63
less ... than 122
like 62, 112
little 121
love 118
lunch 119
made of 111
make 92
make a
(phone) call 128
many 90, 121
map 76
married 77
match 90
matchbox 90
meal 119
mean 67
meat 104
metal 111
milk 110
mine 106
minute 92
miss 77
mobile 128
Monday 112
money 101
month 103
more ... than 95
morning 119
most people 125

mother 78
moving 63
Mr. Brown's 73
much 121
mum 78
next to 125
no = (not any) 100
nobody 71
north 82
not anybody 71
not anything 85
nothing 85
noun 84
o'clock 103
one ... the other 79
only 68
only child 78
only one negative 87
opposite 83, 125
ours 106
out of 96
outside 116
page 62
paper 126
parents 95
Paris 82
past 103
pence 101
pepper 121
phone 128
place 82
plant 117
plastic 111
plate 119
possessive
adjective 105
possessive
pronoun 105
pound 101
prefer 66
preposition 81
present
continuous 53
present simple 56
quantity 120
quarter 75
relations 95
relatives 95
remain 58
repeat 127
rest 125
rice 99
right 63
Rolls Royce 115

Russian	66
salt	121
Saturday	112
school	77
second	92
see	91
she has not / she hasn't	68
side	88
silver	111
similar	92
single	77
singular	120
sister	94
sit down	74
smell	88
some	117
some ... some	85
some of	82
somebody	71
something	85
son	94
south	82
Spanish	75
speak	53
spoon	119
stand up	74
steel	111
still	63
stomach	116
stone	126
street	89
such as	91
sugar	104
Sunday	112
tea	66
teach	75
telephone	128
television	62
tell	65
thank you	67
that	53, 91
that one	127
the fewest	115
the fewest	124
the least	124
the most	109
the one	124
the same ... as	69
theirs	106
they have not / they haven't	68
think	97
Thursday	112
time	103
to	103
to be	113
today	113
tomorrow	113
too	92
top	88
train	77
translation	84
Tuesday	112
ugly	109
uncle	95
up	74
verb	84
walk	73
want	114
was	113
watch	102
water	110
we have not / we haven't	68
wear	64
wearing	64
Wednesday	112
week	103
weekend	112
well	117
west	82
whose	118
why	92
wife	77
will be	113
wine	110
with	64
without	83
wood	126
work	125
year	103
yesterday	113
you don't have	114
you have not / you haven't	68
you have not / you haven't	68
yours	106